You and Me on the Farm:

Barnyard Rules

Me Complete! Curriculum
By Janice Jobey

This book is part of the Me Complete! Early Learning
Program, Volume 2, Unit 4,
"On the Farm" unit.

It may also be used independently.

Please see "Literacy Links" and "Learning
Extensions"in the back of the book for many ways
to engage children in this favorite study topic.

Get Ready to read
"You and Me on the Farm"

* Read the book to simply enjoy the "rules".

* Read the book to find out about how these farm animals show us how to live a healthy, happy life.

* What are some good rules for living a healthy life?

* What are some good rules for getting along with others?

* Use "Literacy Links" in the back of the book to promote literacy skills.

* Use the "Conversational Extenders" throughout the book to enhance thinking skills.

* These farm animals show young children some healthy and happy ways to live. From stretching, drinking water, and grooming all the way to caring and sharing, these delightful farm animals will inspire great conversations for how to get along in this world.

You and me–

So much to do

When we're on the farm!

But these animals are here

With wisdom to share–

From hens to mares,

From brushing your hair

to learning how to share–

We'll learn to care

For both You and Me

And all our friends

On the farm–

Or anywhere!

Conversational Extenders

* What do you think we can learn from farm animals?

Wake up and Stretch!

Wash your Face

Brush your teeth

Conversational Extenders

* Why is it important to brush your teeth? What are other ways to keep our teeth healthy?

Comb your hair

Conversational Extenders

* Why is it important to comb or brush our hair?

Wash your hands often

Conversational Extenders

* Why is it important to wash your hands?

* When should you wash your hands?

* How does this cat wash its paws? How do you wash your hands?

Greet everyone with a smile

Conversational Extenders

* What happens when you smile at someone? How does it make you feel when someone smiles at you?

Eat a good breakfast

Conversational Extenders

* How does a good breakfast prepare you for your day? What is in a healthy breakfast?

Stay with your flock

Conversational Extenders

* Why should you stay with your class? What about when you are on a field trip? What might happen if you didn't?

Listen when the teacher speaks

Put your best foot forward

Conversational Extenders

* Water are some ways you can do this?

Get messy—it's fun!

Clean up after yourself

Conversational Extenders

* How do you clean up after yourself at home? At school?

Take a nap

Conversational Extenders

* Why do our bodies need rest?

Be kind to others

Conversational Extenders

* Why would you need to "bother" the hens?

* A hen can lay an egg every day!

Use helpful words

Conversational Extenders

* What are some helpful words that you know?

Follow your leaders

Conversational Extenders

* Why is it important to stay with your parents or teachers?

Come to circle time

Take turns

Conversational Extenders

* When do you take turns? Why is important to take turns?

Work together

Conversational Extenders

* How do you work together to play or do a job?

Sing like you mean it

Dance, dance, dance!

Help your friends

Conversational Extenders

* What aee some ways to help your friends?

* Do you think this dog might me telling the goat it's time to come inside or to get in line or that is time for lunch? Maybe this goat is coming to help the dog clean up? What do you think?

* What do you say to someone who has helped you?

Drink plenty of water

Conversational Extenders

* Water is important for all of our organs and systems–brain, kidneys, muscles, etc.

* A preschool child needs 5 8-oz glasses every day!

Exercise everyday

Conversational Extenders

* How does exercise keep you strong?

Bathe often

Eat your greens

Conversational Extenders

* What are favorite vegetables? Why is it important to eat a variety of vegetables?

Find the good in others

Conversational Extenders

* How can/do you find the good in others?

Give and receive hugs

Conversational Extenders

* Why are hugs good for you?

Listen to others

Care for others

Conversational Extenders

* How can/do you care for others?

* Why is this important?

And most of all...

Have fun with your friends.

Literacy Links

Read "You and Me on the Farm" to promote literacy!

**Head Start Early Learning Outcomes Framework Preschool Goals are identified in the parenthesis for each strategy below.

1. Pause at each page and have the children predict or guess what lesson the farm animal is teaching. Give hints like, "I think this animal is telling us we should, /b/? That's right, be kind!" Children who think they can "read", will be readers (even if they are reading the picture)! (Goal P-LIT 2)

2. Discuss what letter key words in the text starts with. For example, "'care' begins with the letter 'c". What sound does that make? Who in the class has a name that begins with "c"? Alphabetic Principle allows children to become familiar with letters and their names. (Goal P-LIT 3)

3. Phonemic Awareness can be promoted by having them connect the "sound" of the letter in the words to the alphabet letter. First, make connections of a word on the page to the letter. You might say, "wash" start with /w/ sound…Do you know what letter makes that sound?" You can then ask them to listen for other /w/ sounds in the book. You could also have them identify the letter and sound of the animals or activity on each page. (Goal P-LIT 1, P-LIT 3)

4. Phonological Awareness is not intentionally promoted in this book. However, the reader can use the Phonemic Awareness suggestion above for phonological awareness. Goal P-LIT 1)

5. Read for Comprehension and to expand Vocabulary. Use the Conversational Extenders to connect meanings to their own daily lives. (Goal P-LIT 1)

Learning Connections

Read "You and Me on the Farm" to promote development!

This book's primary focus is self care and social skills.

The Head Start Early Learning Outcomes Framework Preschool Goals supported in reading and using the Conversational Extenders include:

- P-SE 1, 2, 3, 4, 5, 6, 7, 10, 11
- P-ATL 2, 3, 4, 5, 10,
- P-PMP 4, 5, 6

About the Author
Janice S. Jobey, M.S., M.S., CCPS

Janice Jobey is an early childhood expert specializing in literacy, learning, and mental health. Her own childhood experiences with hearing and speech challenges has provided passion in promoting phonological awareness in young children through everyday experiences. Her vast experiences from childhood to "grand-mother-hood" provide the basis for her books and energetic speaking engagements. Janice writes curriculum for infants, toddlers, preschoolers, and parent engagement. Her 35+ years of teaching experience spans from infants to adults and working with children with special needs. She holds graduate degrees in child development and education. She lives in rural Oklahoma where she enjoys writing books and curriculum, spending time in her gardens, and playing with her grandchildren.

Contact Janice Jobey, M.S., M.S., CCPS

janjobey@gmail.com

Find us at

www.earlylearning.today

Facebook@earlyLearningInnovations

Other Titles by Janice Jobey

Me: Learning and Growing

Soft to Touch

My Senses

Just Right

My Hands

Stand Up Tall

Head to Toe

Word Book–Me

Fall and Feelings

Autumn Daze

Autumn Nights

10 Little Blackbirds

One Little Leaf

Scarecrow Scarecrow/Scarecrow Moves

Word Book–Fall and Feelings

Family Love

Oh Grana!

Oh Poppa!

Snug as a Bug

Dancing On Daddy's Shoes

Rocking in Mama's Arms

We Believe!

Spring Set

Flower Garden ABC

Spring Shorts

Spring Senses

12 Little Ducks

Word Book-Spring

Me and My Family

A Family Needs Love

My Family

I'm Thankful

Word Book–Family

Me and You

Rules Keep Us Safe

Just Look at My Face

Healing Hearts

These 3 Things

Me Without You

Some Day

Woodland Wonder

Woodland Riddles

Woodland ABC's

Fox in the City

Racoon and Loon

10 Striped Skunks

Wild Summer Nights

Woodland Moves

Word Book

Healthy Me

Eat The Rainbow

Healthy Habits

Bears and Teddy Bears
Hivey Goes to Town
Harvey Goes Camping
55 Hungry Bears
B is for Bear
Bears WORD book
Bears Everywhere
Can You Be a Bear?
Word Book–Bears

Pet Set
Pet ABCs
Pet Riddles
Pig Prince
Pet Shop
Word Book–Pets

Winter Time
Things I like About Winter
Frost
Snow Echo
Secret Season
1 Little Snowflake
W is for Winter
Word Book–Winter Time

Me and My Friends
20 Little Friends
My Friends are Just Right
Bee-Attitude Friends
Being Friendly
Word Book–Me and My Friends

On the Farm
F is for Farm
Barnyard Riddles
Barnyard Chores
Barnyard Chant
Hen and Chicks
Turkey Turley Finds His Gobble
Word Book–Farm
You and Me on the Farm
Barnyard Groove

Many People, One Country
Pledge of Allegiance
America the Beautiful
This Land is Your Land
One to Many
On My Way to the Parade
WORD book

Pretend Fun
A Princess Needs a Crown
A Pirate Needs a Hat

Made in the USA
Middletown, DE
09 August 2024

58588774R00024